Mel Bay's

DELUXE
Tinwhistle Songbook

By Patrick Conway

2

TABLE OF CONTENTS

BASIC TINWHISTLE INFORMATION
How To Play The Tinwhistle 4
Notes On The Tinwhistle 5
Holding The Tinwhistle 6
Rudiments of Music 7
Ledger Lines and Notes 8
Bar Lines and Repeats 9
Time Signatures 10
Ornamentation . . . . 11 and 13

IRISH BALLADS
Báidín Fheidhlimid 14
Beir Mé Ó 15
The Dawning Of The Day 16
Home Boys Home 17
Shores of Amerikay 18
The Meeting Of The Waters 19
Londonderry Air 20
The Holy Ground 22
The Spanish Lady 23
Whiskey In The Jar 24
Sí Beag Sí Mór 25

Spancil Hill 26
Roddy McCorley 27
Dicey Reilly 28
The Minstrel Boy 29
Brennan On The Moor 30
Old Maid In A Garret 31
'Tis The Last Rose Of Summer 32
The Ould Orange Flute 33
Believe Me If All Those Endearing Young
    Charms 34
The Rising Of The Moon 35
The Golden Jubilee 36
Cockles and Mussels 37
The Wild Rover 38
The Merry Plow Boy 39
The Galway Shawl 40
The Wild Colonial Boy 41
The Foggy Dew 42
The Old Woman From Wexford 43
The Sally Gardens 44
The Butcher Boy 45
Love Is Teasin' 46

The Galway Races 47
I'll Tell Me Ma 48

HORNPIPES
The Greencastle 50
The Liverpool Hornpipe 51
The Harvest Home 52
The Boys of Blue Hill 53
Dumphy's Hornpipe 54
The Kildare Hornpipe 55
The Stack of Barley 56
Julia's Wedding 57
Liz Coffey's Drake 58

JIGS
Haste To The Wedding 60
The Hare In The Corn 61
The Humors of Bandon 62
Father O'Flynn 63
The Connaughts Man's Rambles 64
Life Is All Checquered 65
The Frost Is All Over 66
Saint Kevin's Bed 67

Pet Of The Pipers 68
Smash The Windows 69
Terry's Fancy 70
The Ten Penny Bit 71
Saddle The Pony 72
The Rocky Road To Dublin 73
St. Patrick's Day 74
The Irish Washerwoman 75

REELS
Drowsy Maggie 77
Miss McLeod's Reel 78
The Smithfield Haymen 79
The Green Meadow 80
The Wind That Shakes The Barley 81
The Pigeon On The Gate 82
The Merry Blacksmith 83
The Flowing Bowl 84
Bonnie Kate 85
The Green Groves of Erin 86
The Blackberry Blossom 87
The Rakes of Mallow 88

How To Play The Tinwhistle

NOTATION

o   These spots and circles represent the Tin Whistle.
o   The spots indicate the fingers to be placed on the whistle.
o   The circles indicate the holes to be left open.
●
●
●

A half filled circle ◓ represents a half-tone. The finger should be placed on the top half of the hole only.

+   This cross indicates that the note is played in the upper octave. This may be obtained by blowing somewhat stronger.

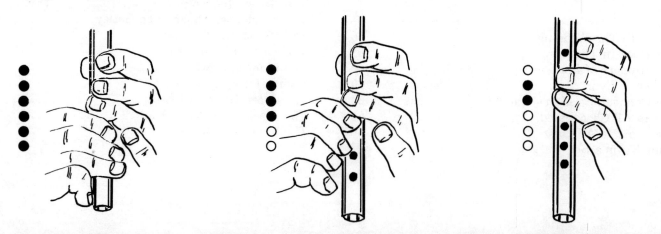

Notes On The Tinwhistle

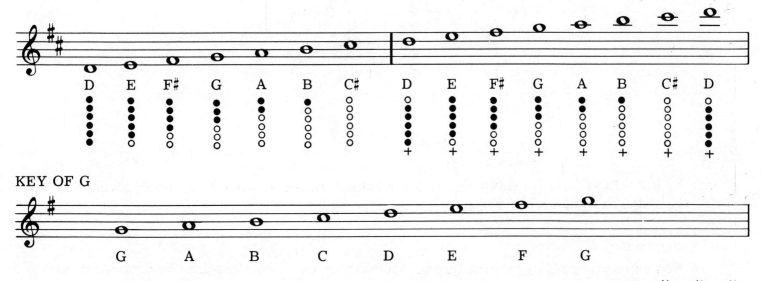

The note of C Natural (C♮) on the D whistle may be fingered in the three following ways:

Holding The Tinwhistle

HOLDING

The tin whistle rests on both thumbs, which are placed underneath. The little fingers which are not used for playing notes are placed on either side.

IMPORTANT : Always make sure that the holes that are stopped (this means covered or closed) are completely covered.

BLOWING

Notes are produced by blowing through the mouthpiece. Two notes may be obtained from the same hole.

To get the notes on the lower octave you only need to breathe or blow gently through the mouthpiece.

The notes on the upper octave may be obtained by blowing somewhat stronger. In either case it is important to maintain a steady air flow.

Music is written by means of signs or symbols, called notation after the first seven letters of the alphabet:

A B C D E F G

These notes are written on five horizontal lines and between four spaces called the STAVE or STAFF.

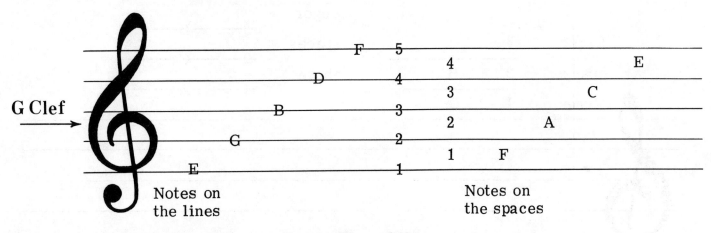

G Clef

Notes on
the lines

Notes on
the spaces

Note: It is important to memorise the position of these notes. The notes on the lines may be learned more easily by memorising the following:

<u>E</u>very <u>G</u>ood <u>B</u>oy <u>D</u>eserves <u>F</u>avours

and the space notes - F A C E (face)

Ledger Lines and Notes

LEGER NOTES are an exiension of the staff. These are
short horizontal lines which are placed above and below
the stave when required. Below is an example of leger
notes written thus:

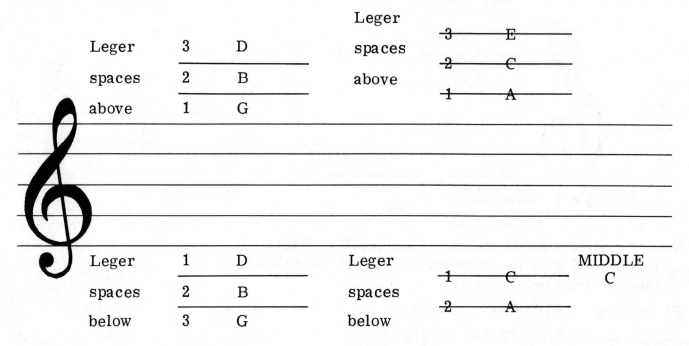

Bar Lines and Repeats

Music is divided into equal periods of time by means of Bar Lines.

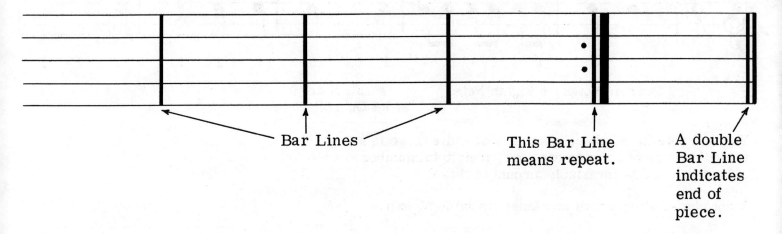

Bar Lines

This Bar Line means repeat.

A double Bar Line indicates end of piece.

Time Signatures

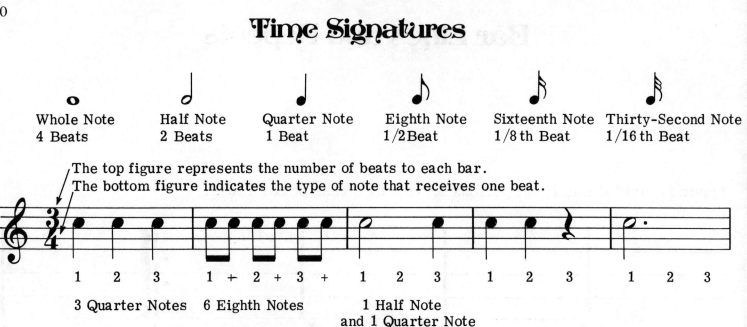

Whole Note — 4 Beats   Half Note — 2 Beats   Quarter Note — 1 Beat   Eighth Note — 1/2 Beat   Sixteenth Note — 1/8 th Beat   Thirty-Second Note — 1/16 th Beat

The top figure represents the number of beats to each bar.
The bottom figure indicates the type of note that receives one beat.

3 Quarter Notes   6 Eighth Notes   1 Half Note and 1 Quarter Note

You will note in the above example that while there is a varied number of notes to each bar, their total number of beats or counts invariably amount to three.

A dot placed after a note increases its value by half.

Ornamentation

VIBRATO

This quivering effect on the notes may be obtained by tapping rapidly on the whistle.

For example; for the note of G tap rapidly on the F# hole.

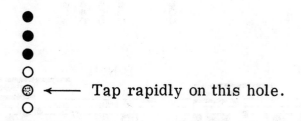 ←——— Tap rapidly on this hole.

This method is very effective when playing slow airs.

Ornamentation

ROLLING

This method is used by most of the Irish Players. It is quite difficult to learn but once mastered proves well worth the effort.

The last four notes which are joined together are played very quickly with a reflex action.

E Roll

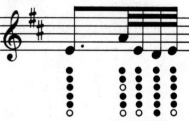

F♯ Roll

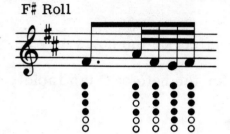

G Roll   A Roll   B Roll

Irish Ballads

Báidín Fheidhilmid

Beir Mé Ó

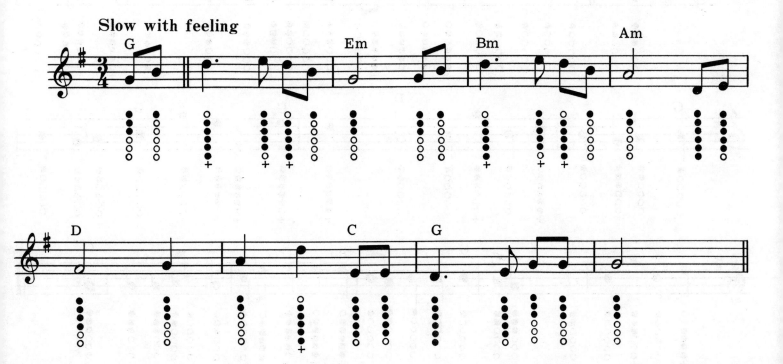

The Dawning Of The Day

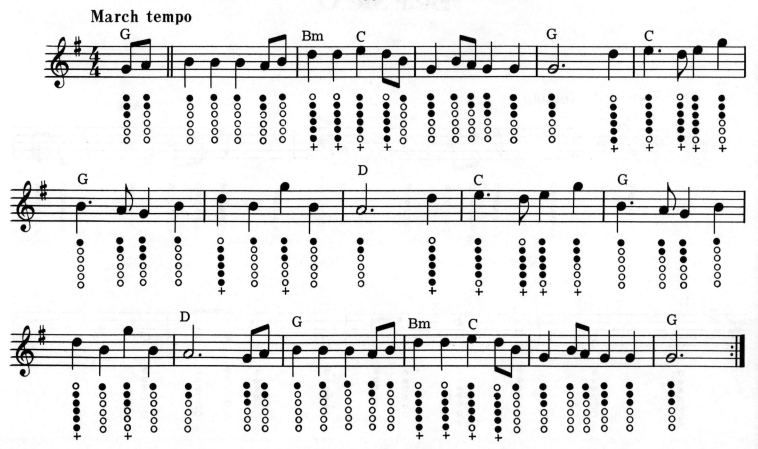

Home Boys Home

Shores of Amerikay

The Meeting Of The Waters

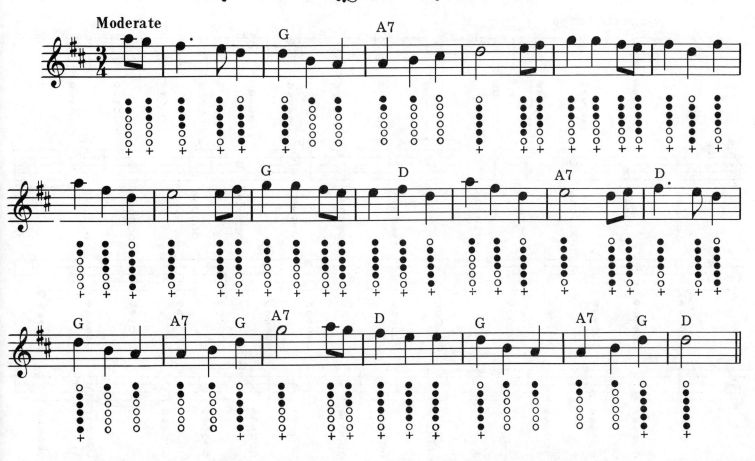

The Londonderry Air

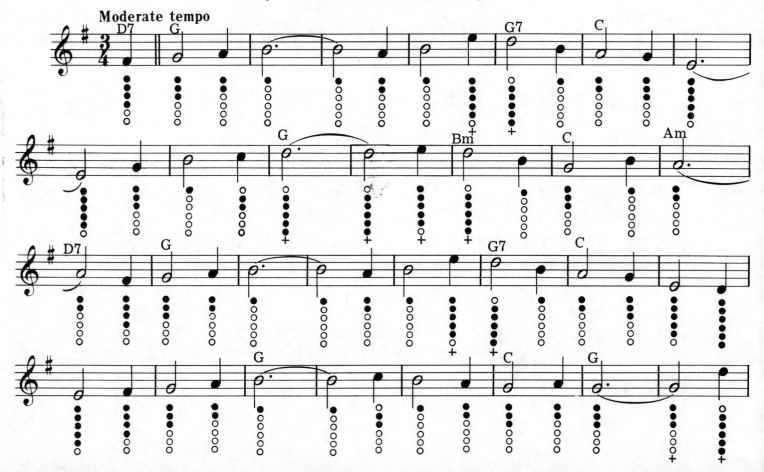

21

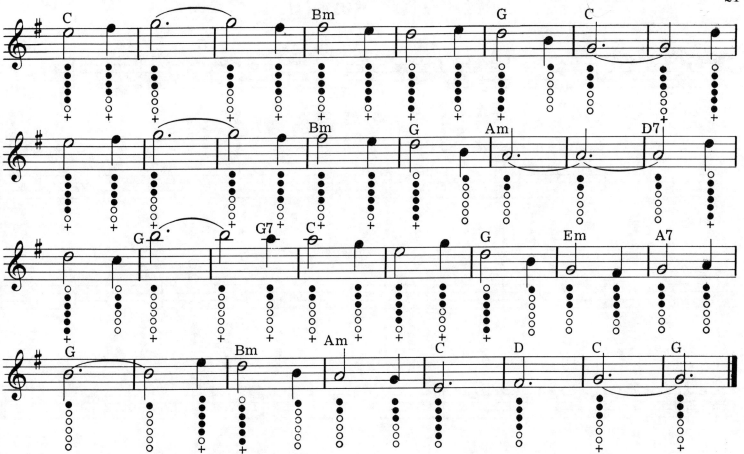

The Holy Ground

Fast and lively

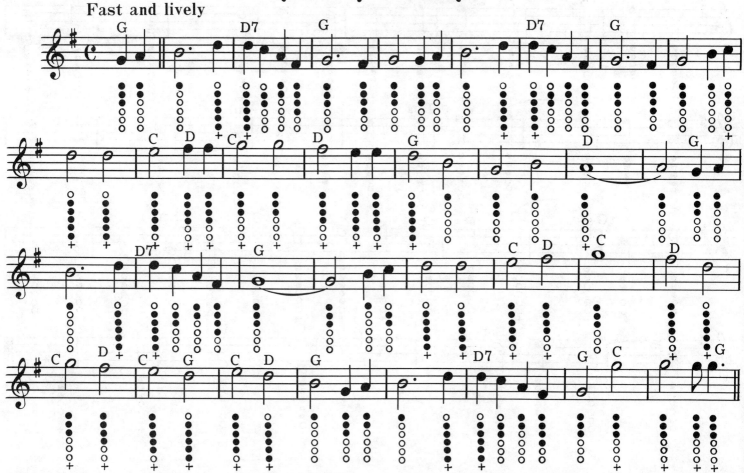

The Spanish Lady

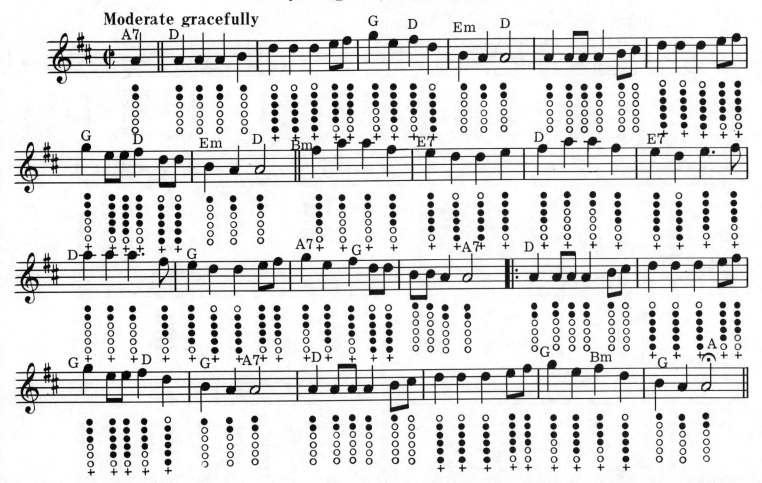

Whiskey In The Jar

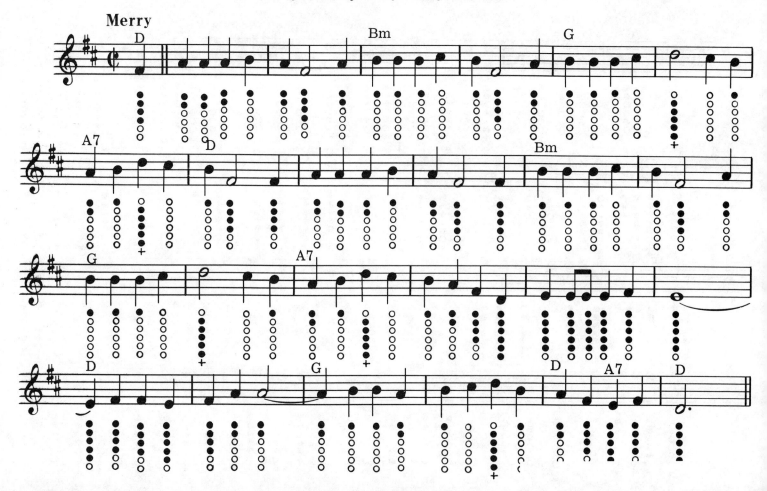

Sí Beag Sí Mór

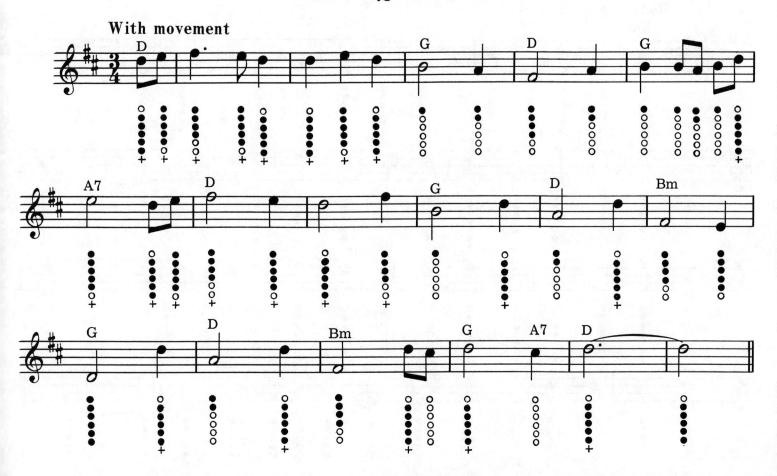

Spancil Hill

Moderate with feeling

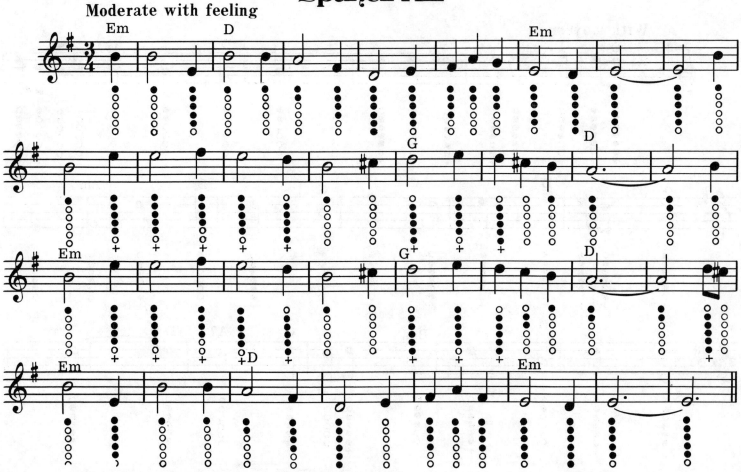

Roddy McCorley

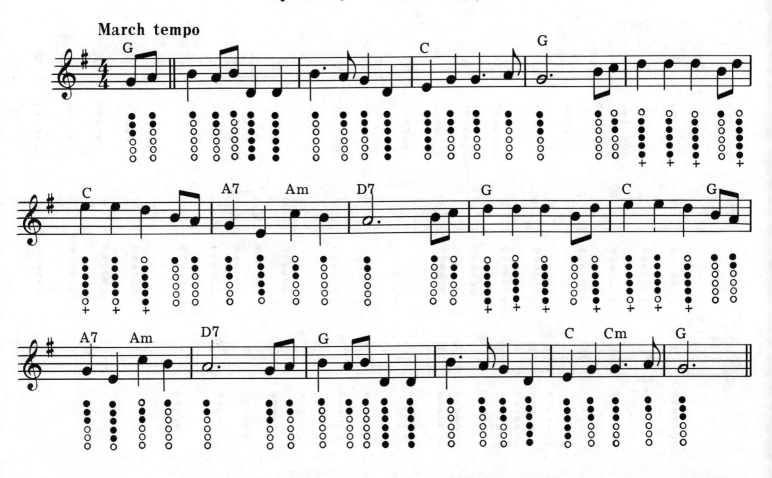

Dicey Reilly

Merry

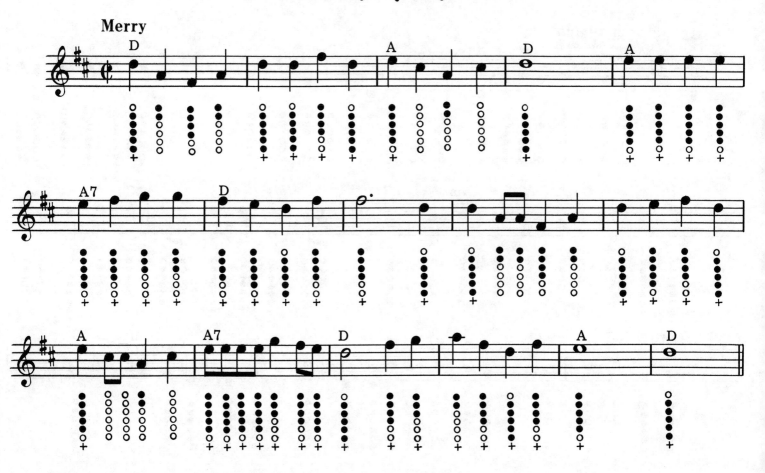

The Minstrel Boy

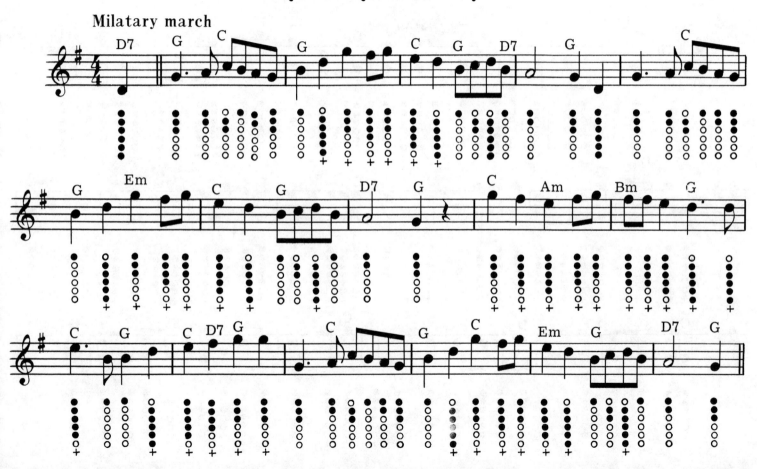

Brennan On The Moor

Old Maid In A Garret

'Tis The Last Rose Of Summer

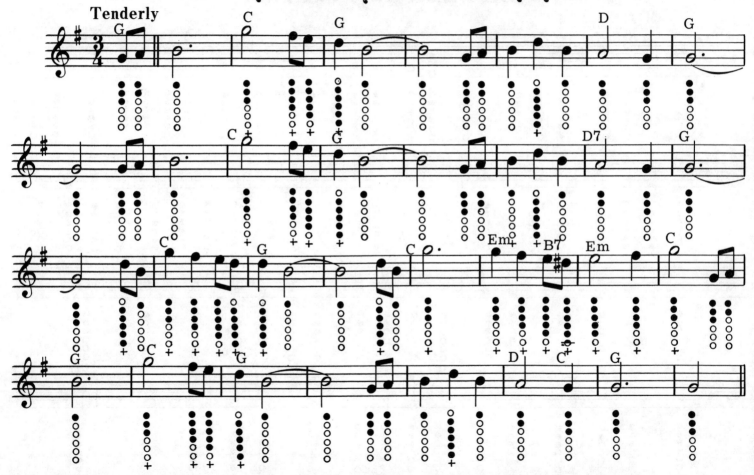

The Ould Orange Flute

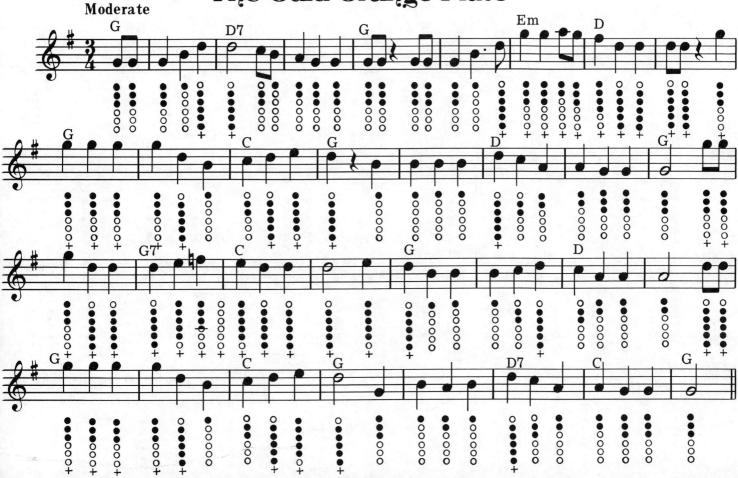

Believe Me If All Those Endearing Young Charms

Slow with feeling

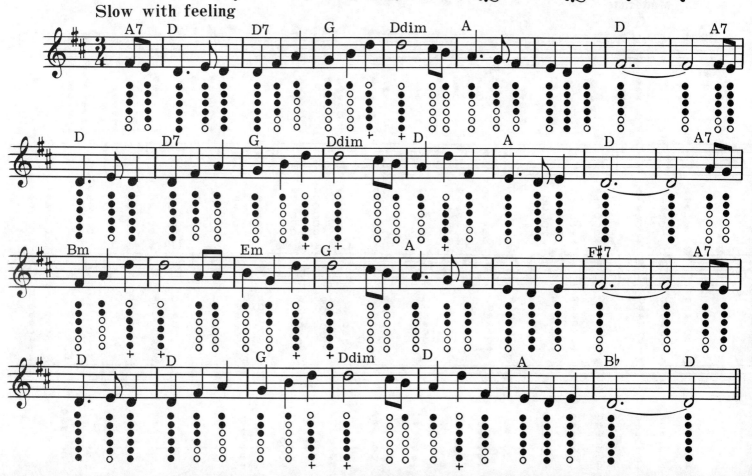

The Rising Of The Moon

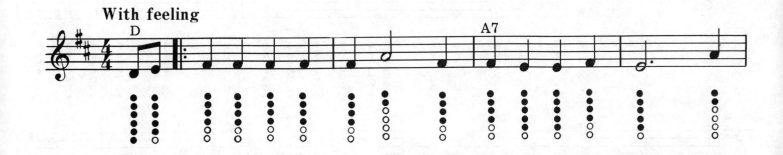

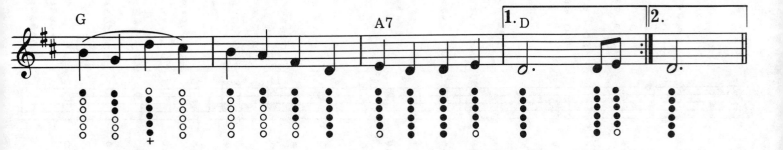

The Golden Jubilee

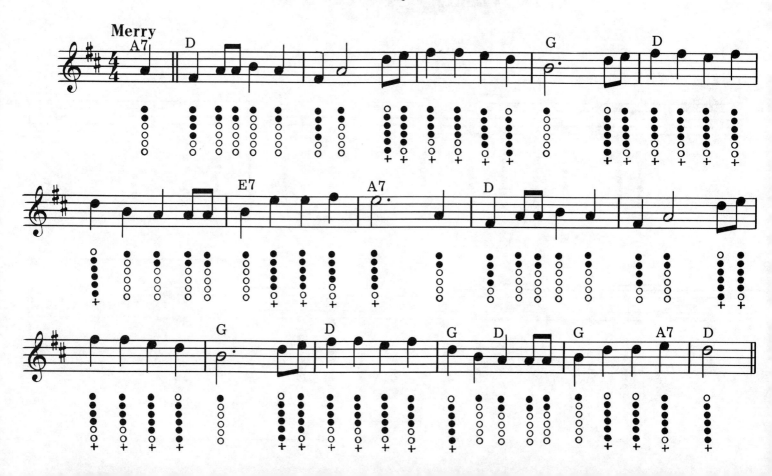

Cockles and Mussels

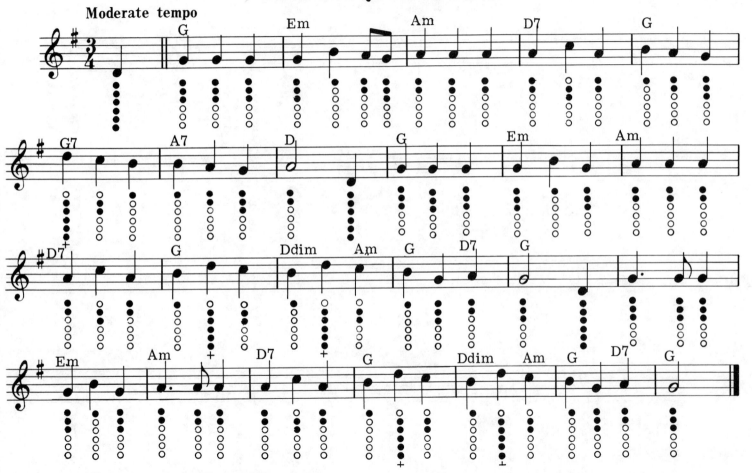

The Wild Rover

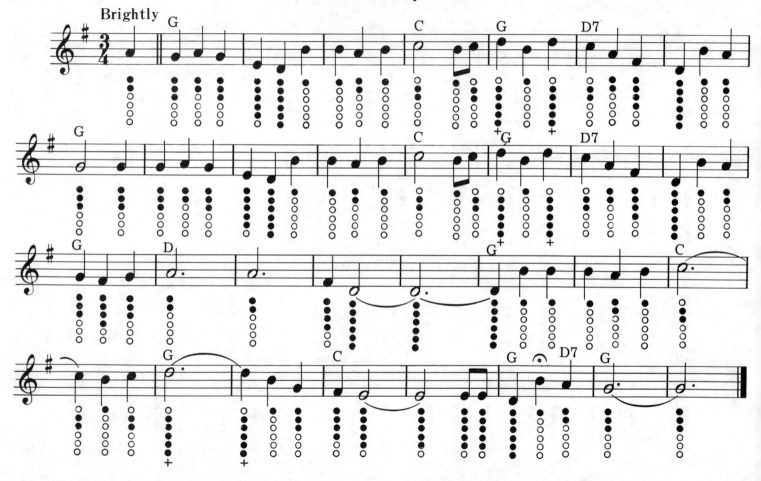

The Merry Plowboy

The Galway Shawl

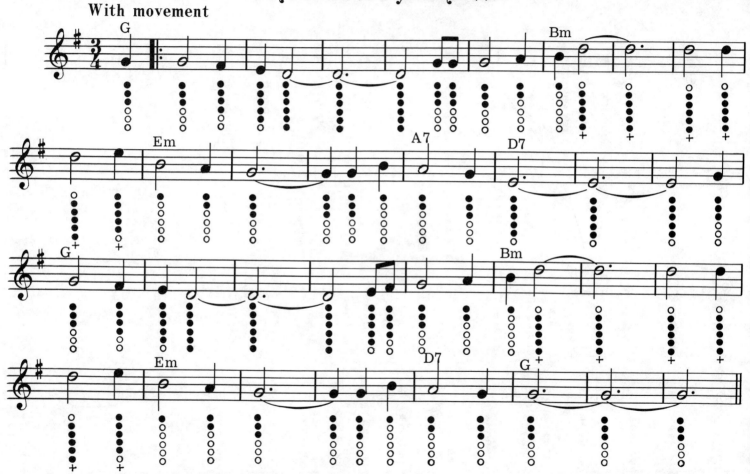

The Wild Colonial Boy

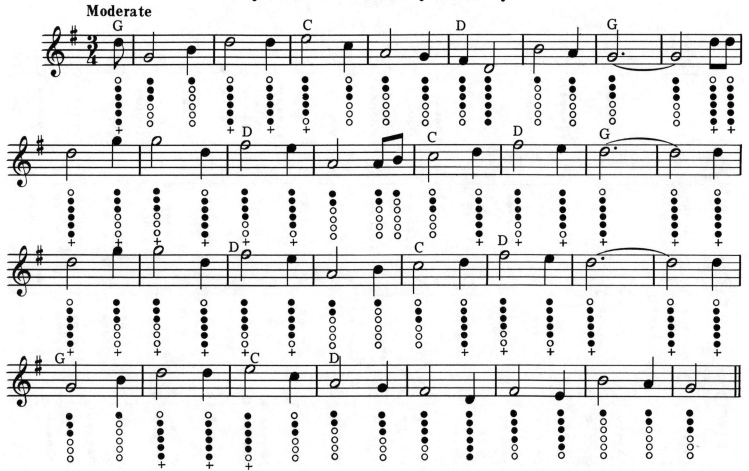

The Foggy Dew

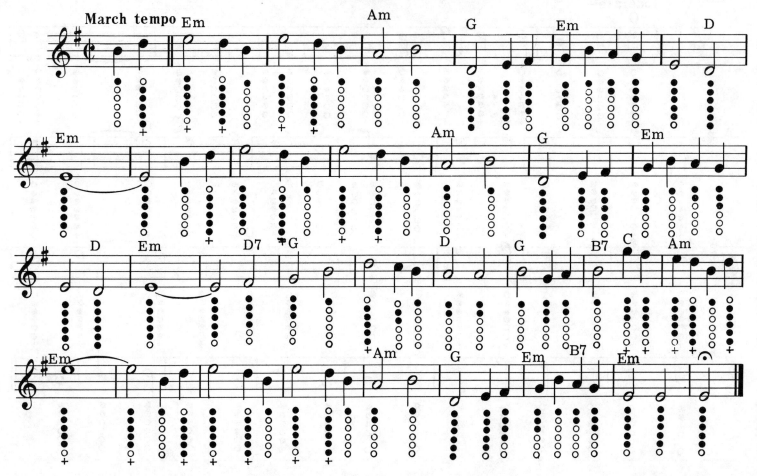

The Old Woman From Wexford

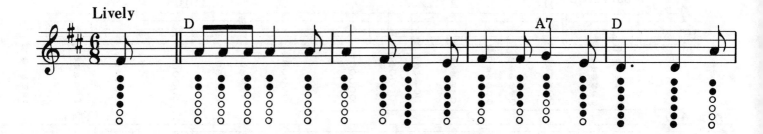

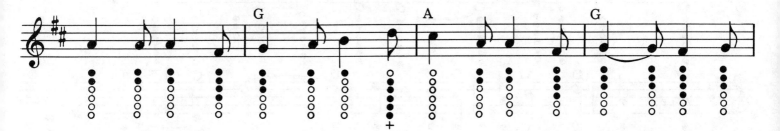

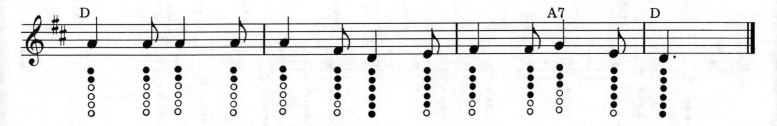

The Sally Gardens

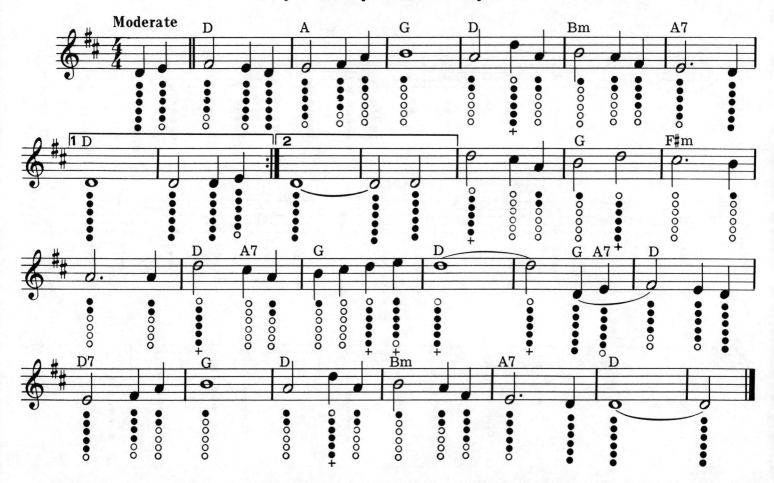

The Butcher Boy

Slow with feeling

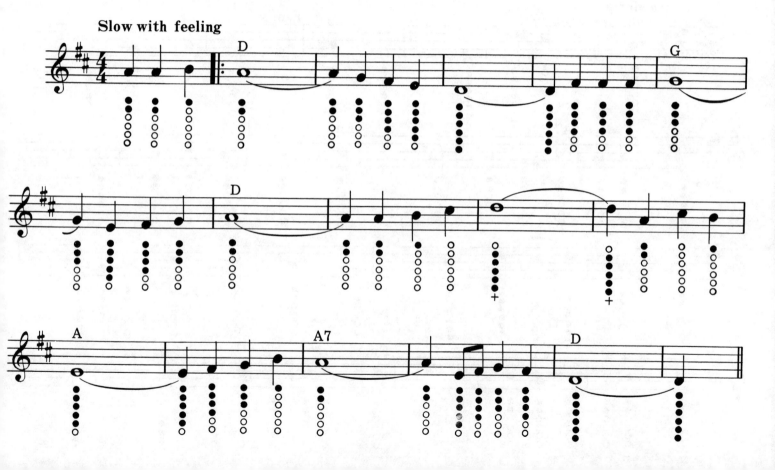

Love Is Teasin'

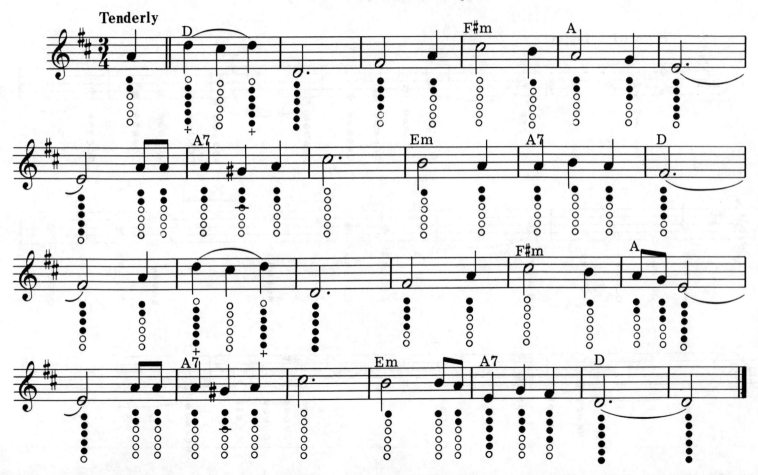

The Galway Races

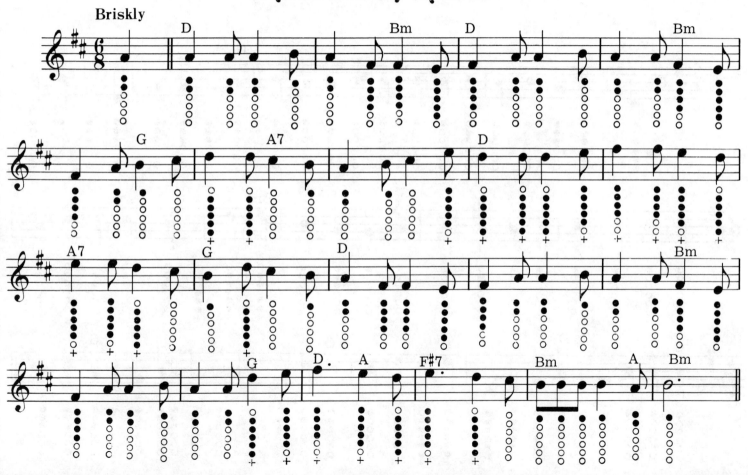

I'll Tell Me Ma

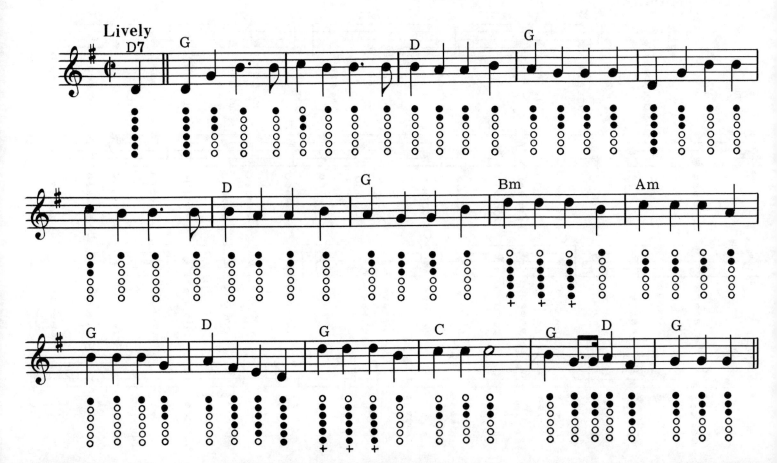

Hornpipes

The Greencastle

Bright with spirit

Hornpipe

The Liverpool Hornpipe

Bright with spirit

Hornpipe

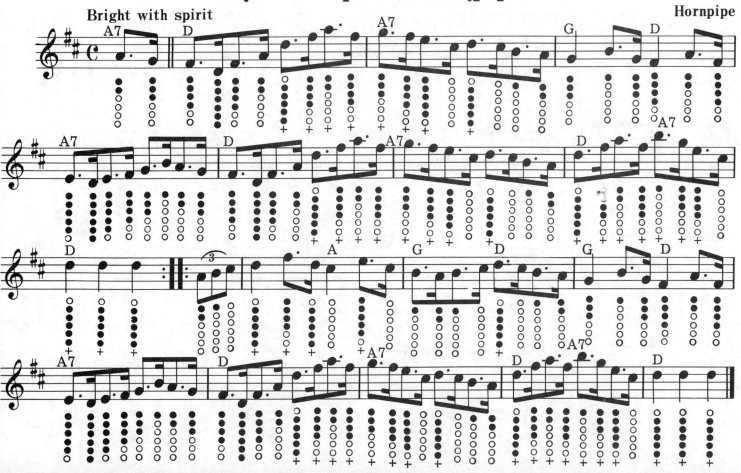

The Harvest Home

Hornpipe

Bright with spirit

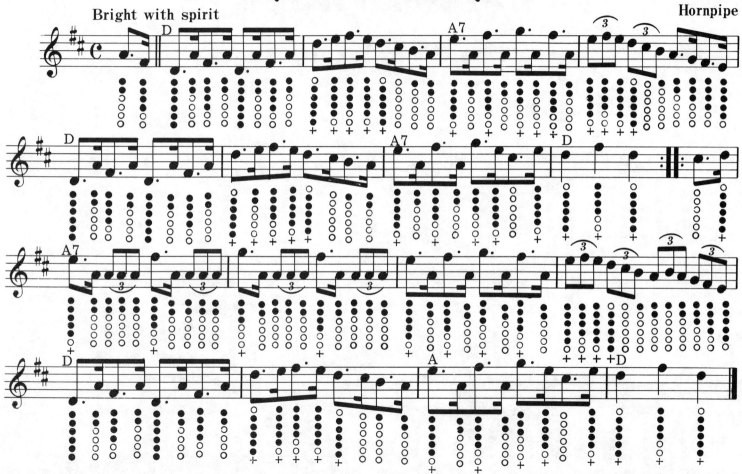

The Boys of Blue Hill

Bright with spirit

Hornpipe

Dumphy's Hornpipe

Bright with spirit

Hornpipe

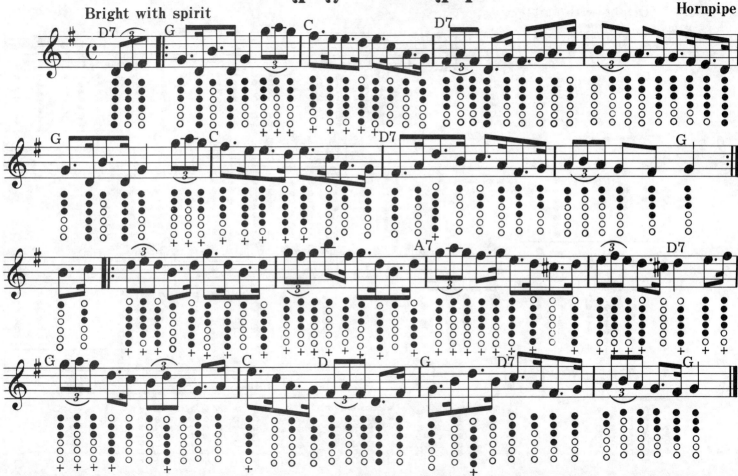

The Kildare Hornpipe

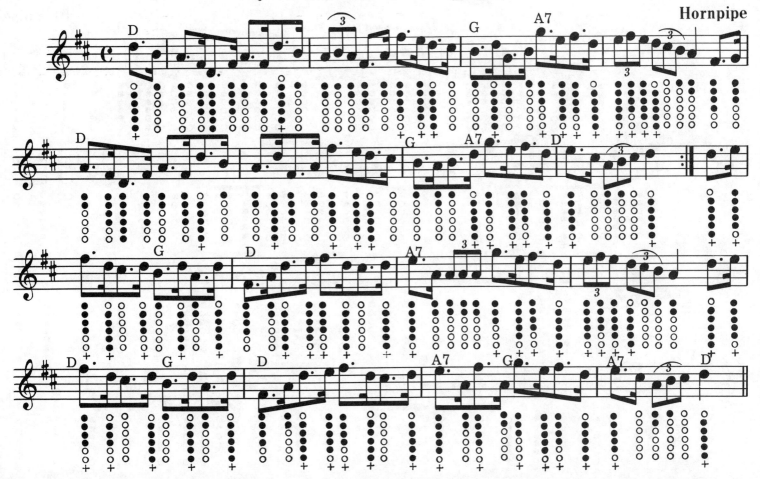

The Stack of Barley

Julia's Wedding

Hornpipe

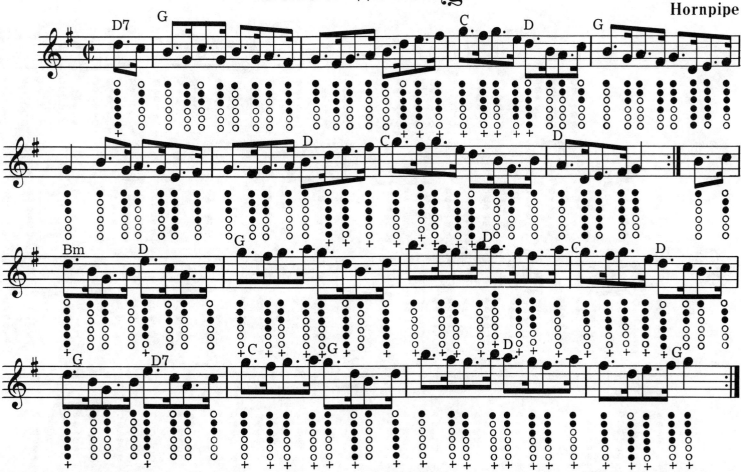

Liz Coffey's Drake

Hornpipe

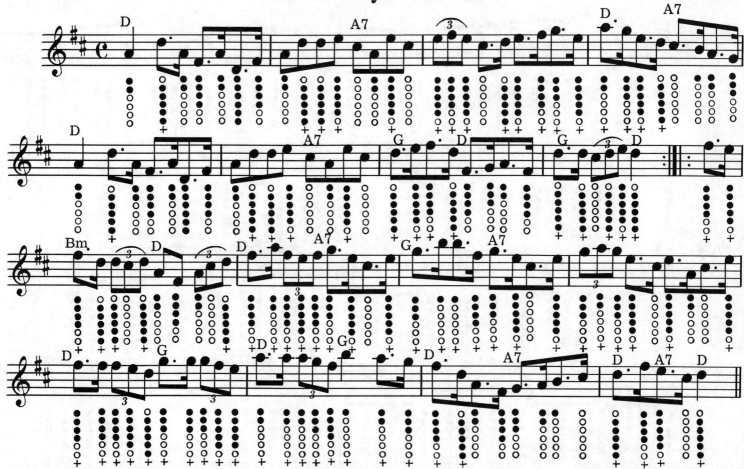

Jigs

Haste To The Wedding

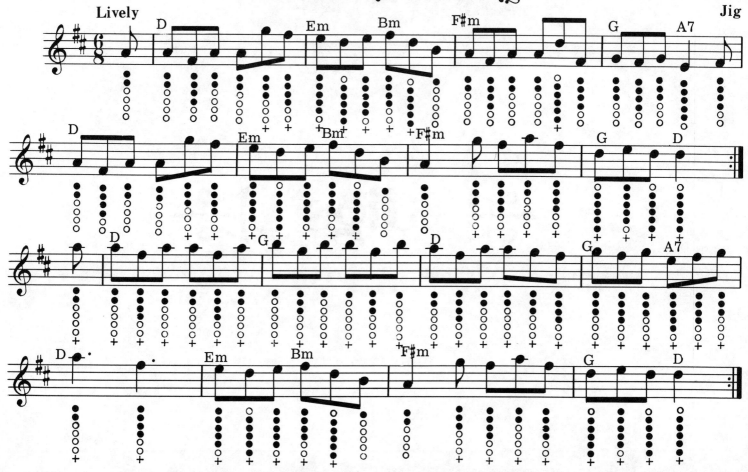

The Hare In The Corn

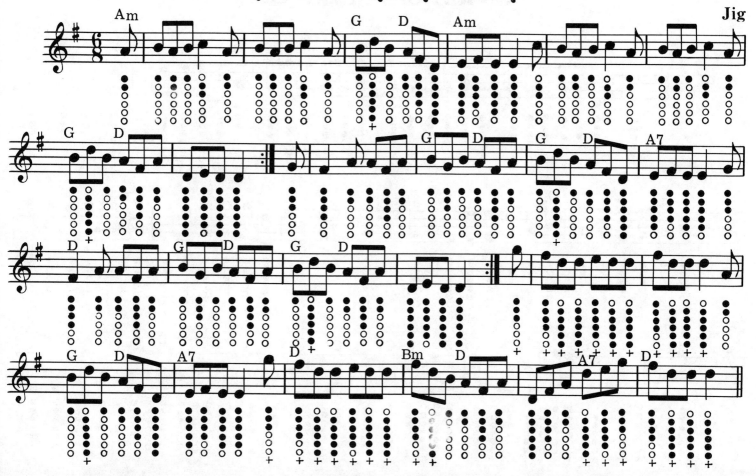

The Humors of Bandon

Jig

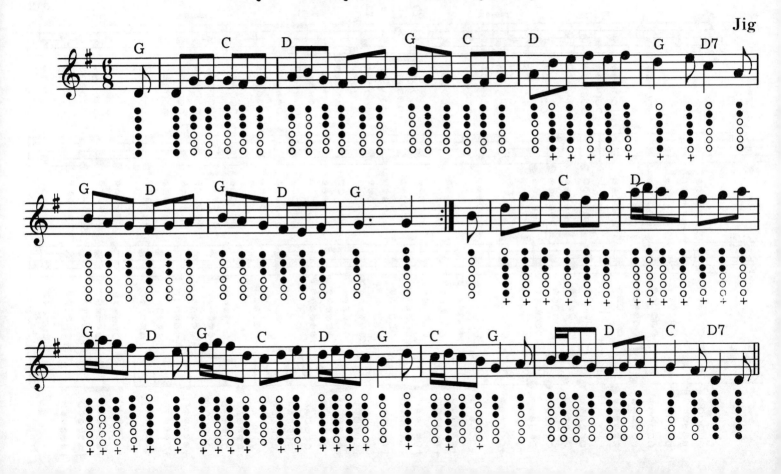

Father O'Flynn

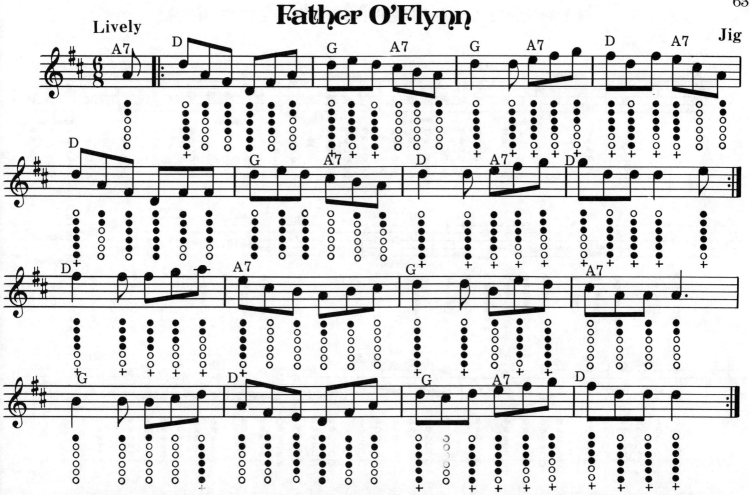

The Connaughts Man's Rambles

Jig

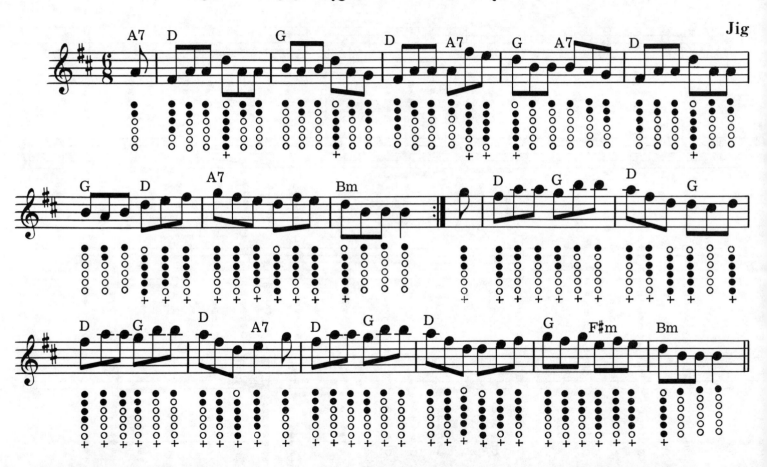

Life Is All Checquered

The Frost Is All Over

Jig

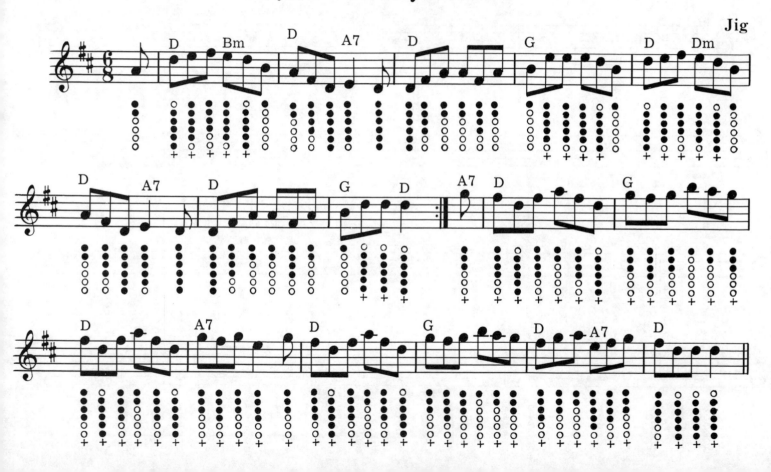

Saint Kevin's Bed

Jig

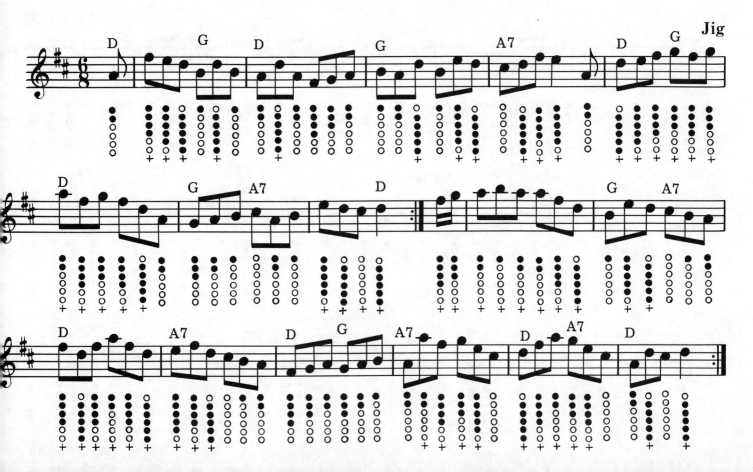

Pet Of The Pipers

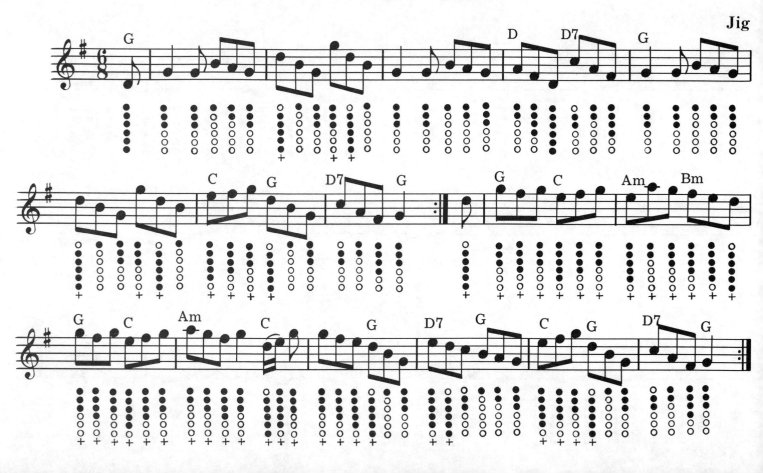

Smash The Windows

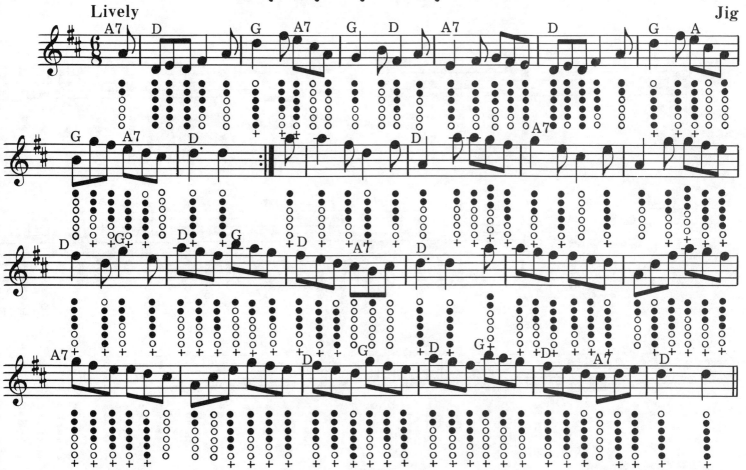

Terry's Fancy

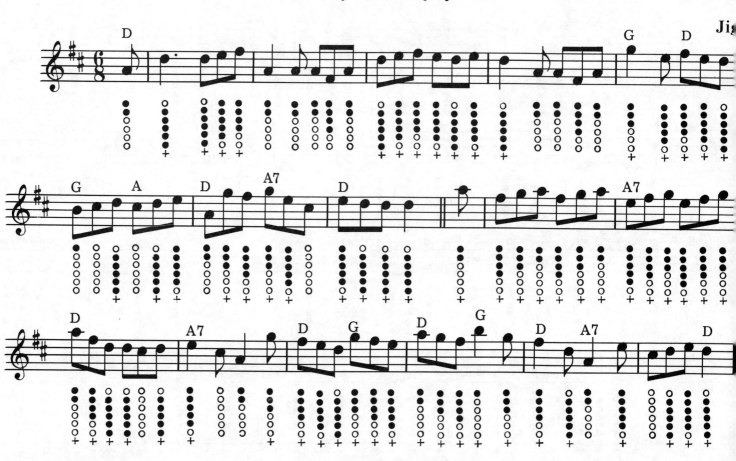

The Ten Penny Bit

71

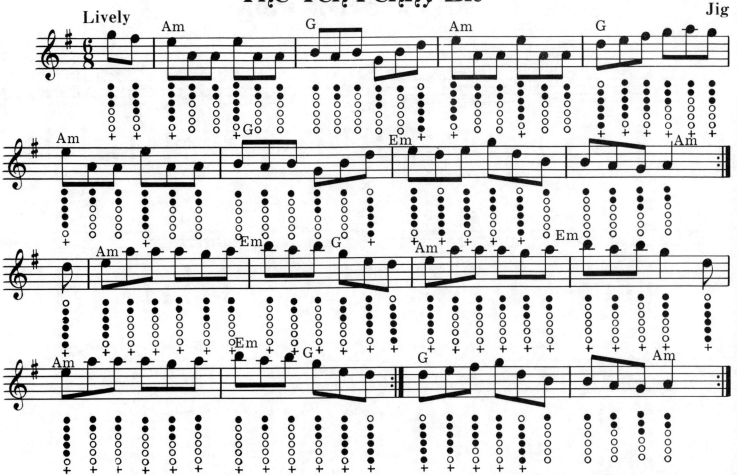

72

Saddle The Pony

Jig

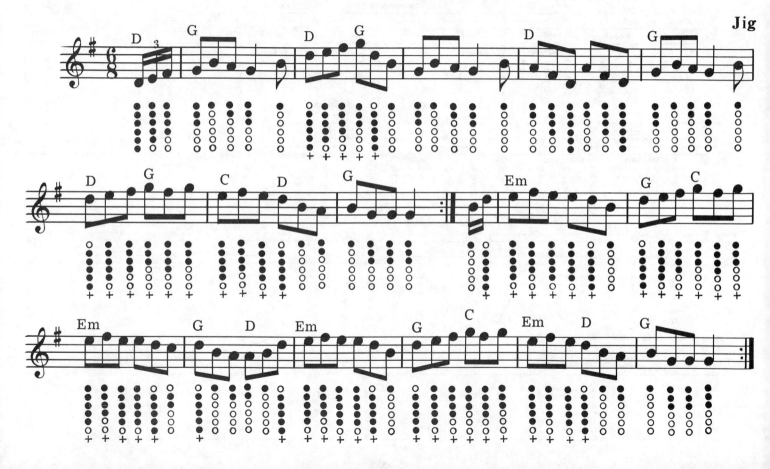

The Rocky Road To Dublin

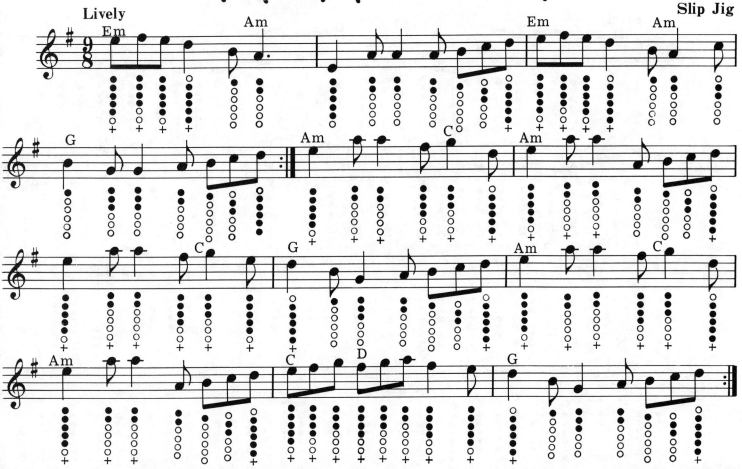

St. Patrick's Day

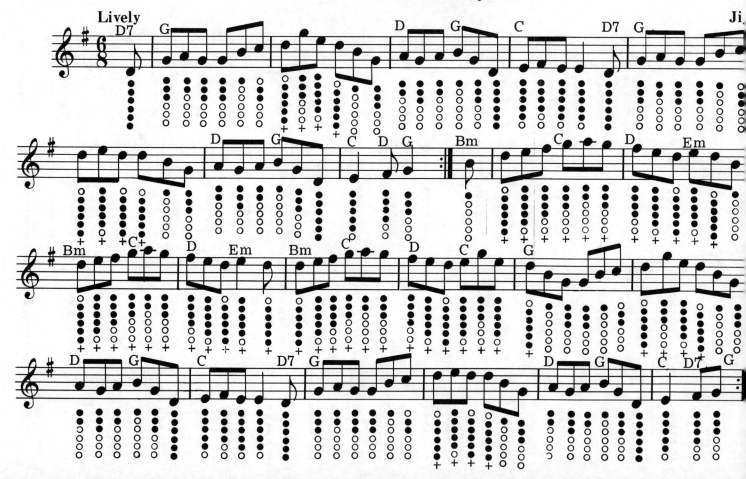

The Irish Washerwoman

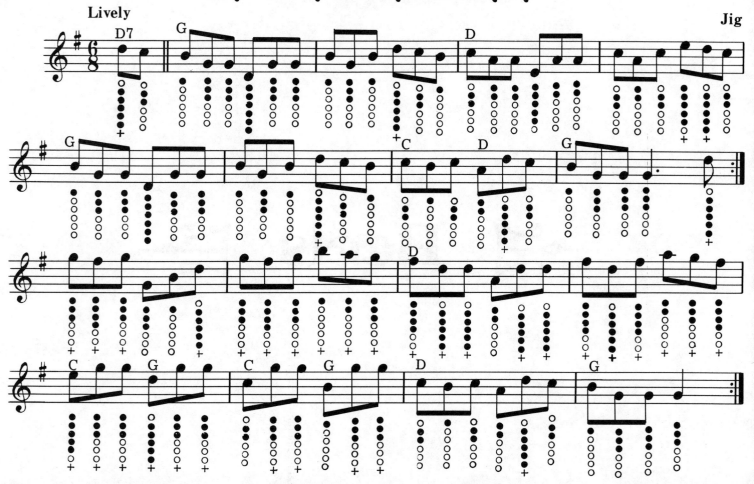

Reels

Drowsy Maggie

Reel

Miss McLeod's Reel

Lively

Reel

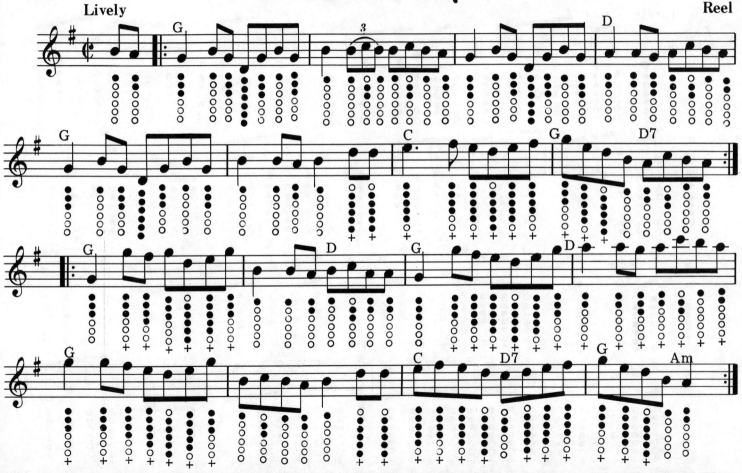

The Smithfield Haymen

Reel

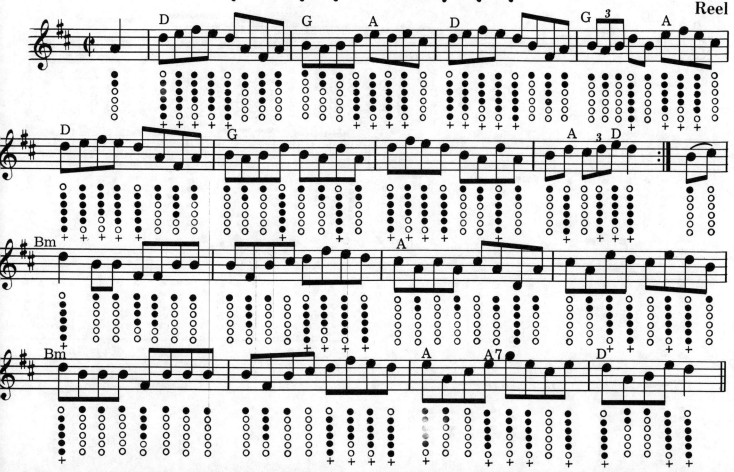

The Green Meadow

Reel

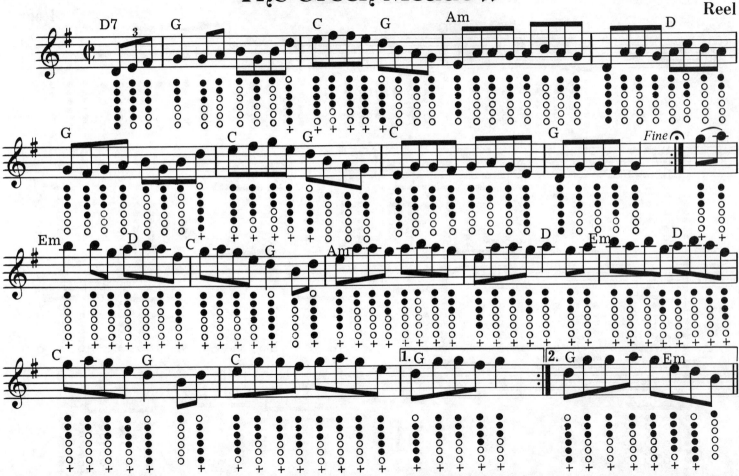

The Wind That Shakes The Barley

Reel

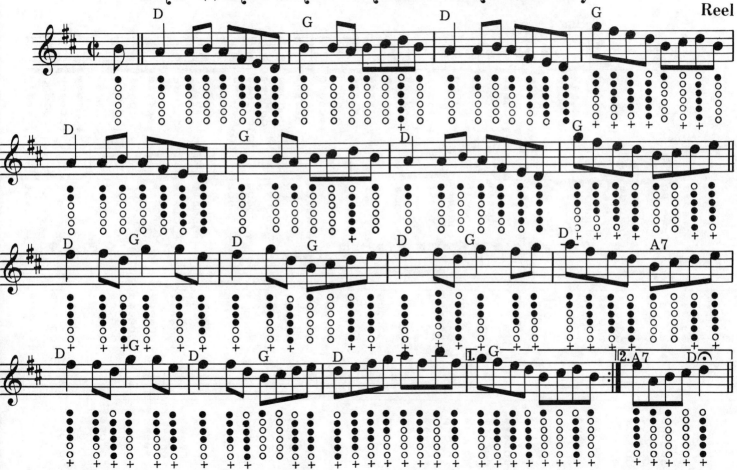

The Pigeon On The Gate

Reel

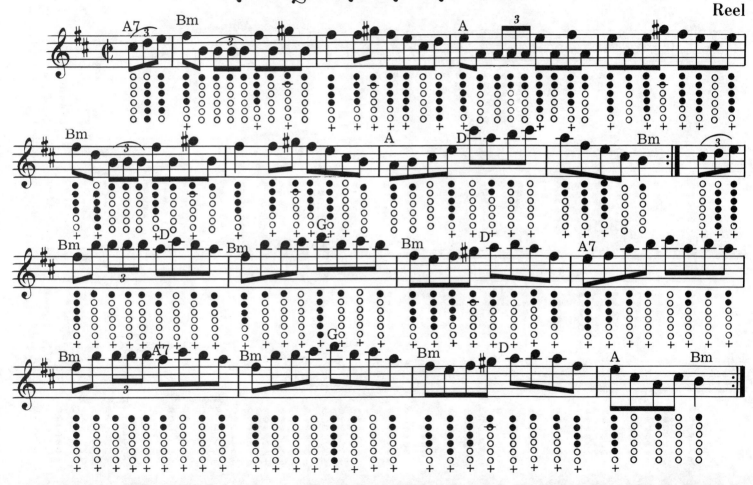

The Merry Blacksmith

The Flowing Bowl

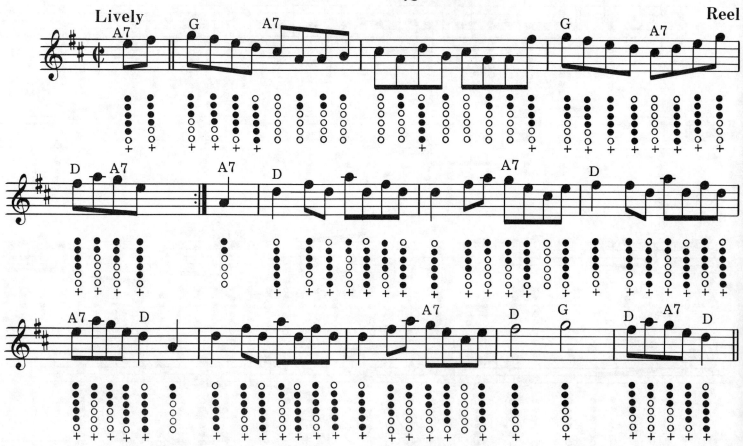

Bonnie Kate

Reel

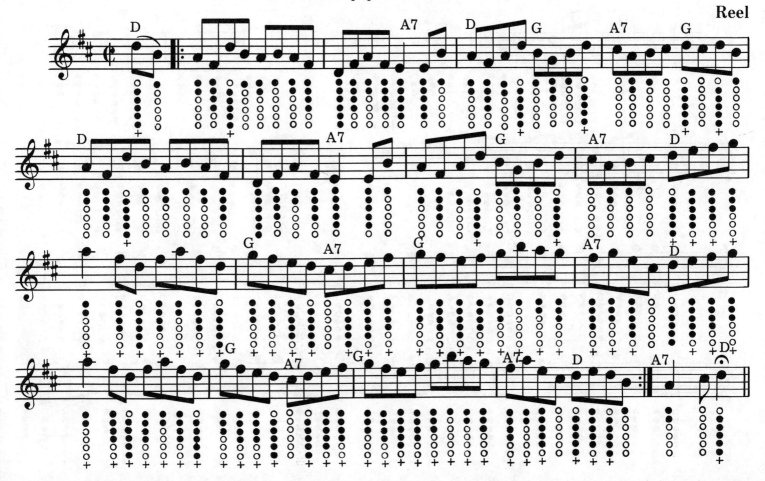

The Green Groves of Erin

Reel

The Blackberry Blossom

Reel

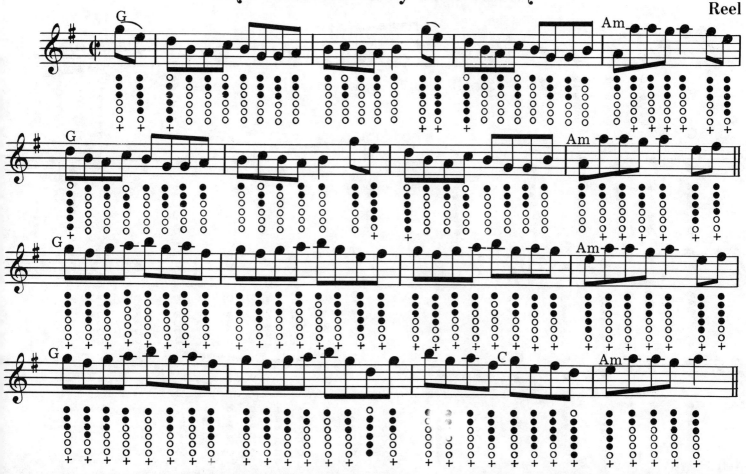

The Rakes of Mallow

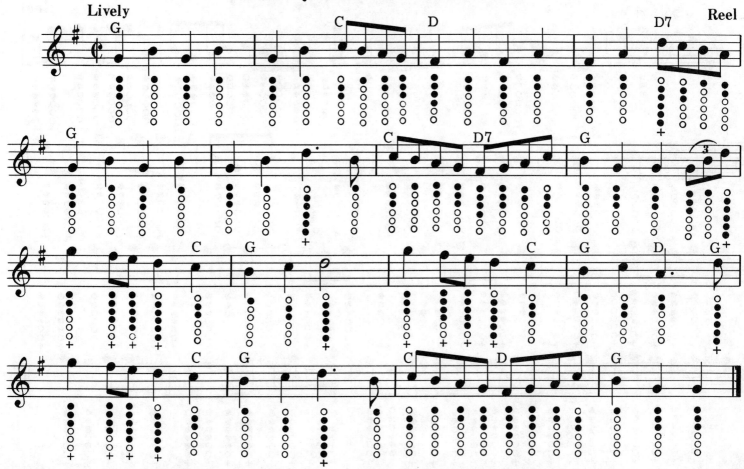